ICEBERGS

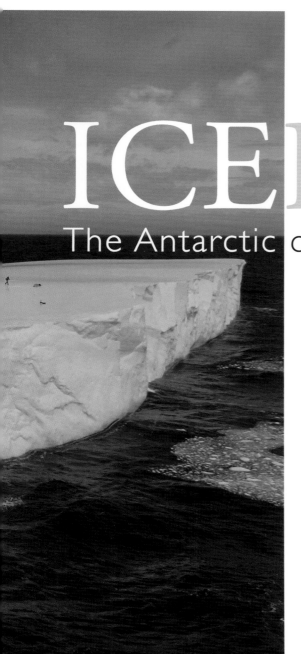

ICEBERGS

The Antarctic comes to town DAVE CULL

Photographs by Stephen Jaquiery

Otago Daily Times

Longacre Press

Otago Daily Times

Longacre Press thanks the *Otago Daily Times* for their co-operation and support.

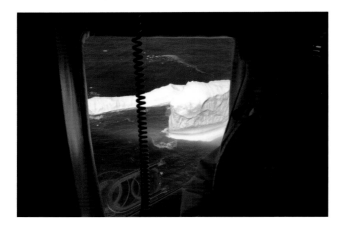

Acknowledgements:

Author, Dave Cull

Exploring and then writing up the journey of our visiting icebergs, turned into my own journey of exploration. Along the way a number of people were extremely helpful. In particular Dr Pat Langhorne of the University of Otago, who pointed out an alternative path of enquiry, at the end of which I found John Dunbier, without whose generous assistance I simply could not have completed my story. Thankyou both.

I'm also grateful to Peter Barrett of Victoria University of Wellington, Wolfgang Rack of the University of Canterbury and Mike Williams of NIWA for timely information and pointers.

Thanks also to the various people who took the time to speak to me of their experiences on or above the bergs.

Finally a tribute to Stephen Jaquiery's magnificent photographs. They speak for themselves.

Photographer, Stephen Jaquiery

Thank-you to Graeme Gale and his team at Helicopters Otago Ltd. Without Graeme's generosity and enthusiasm many of the iceberg photographs would not have been possible. And without that "Southern, Kiwi-can-do attitude" of both Graeme Gale and Richard Hayes of Southern Lakes Helicopters, we would never have been able to take Shrek out to such a unique location to be shorn.

Text © Dave Cull

Photos © *Otago Daily Times* except where otherwise credited
Illustrations and maps: *Otago Daily Times*

Photographs are by Stephen Jaquiery except where otherwise credited

ISBN 978 1 877361 94 4

A catalogue record for this book is available from the National Library of New Zealand.

First published by Longacre Press, 2007
30 Moray Place, Dunedin, New Zealand.

Book design and cover design by Christine Buess
Printed by Printlink, Wellington

www.longacre.co.nz

To purchase the *Otago Daily Times* iceberg images visit
www.otagoimages.co.nz

Otago Daily Times report: 4 NOVEMBER 2006.

'About 100 icebergs, in two groups, have been found south of New Zealand with the first group no more than 262 km south of Invercargill.

The size of the largest iceberg was about 2 km by 1.5 km and more than 130 m high. A Royal New Zealand Air Force Orion aircraft on a fisheries patrol spotted the huge sheets of ice.' NZPA

Over the next month, several icebergs would drift north along the South Island coast, and for the first time since 1931 icebergs were visible from mainland New Zealand.

They were magnificent: stately, graceful, apparently timeless but constantly changing. And like migrating birds, just as we had become acquainted with them, they moved on.

Where did they come from, and how old were they?

❆   ❆   ❆

Antarctic mountains. © G BLICK, ANTARCTICA NZ PICTORIAL COLLECTION K450 03/04

Origins

Whirling snow flails the darkness then settles in a fine, powdery layer over an endless white slope. There hasn't been a sunrise for months and it's a deadly -70°C. Not a creature stirs for hundreds of kilometres – certainly not humans. They won't arrive here for millions of years. The millennia tick by like a metronome's chant, while blizzard upon blizzard scatters its crystal seed.

This is the coldest, driest, highest and windiest continent on planet Earth, and its largest desert. It never rains here. Any moisture that falls is snow: barely 10 cm each year. And it never melts. Over millions of long winters and brief summers the snow just gets deeper. From its granular form known as 'névé' it is gradually transformed, by the weight of countless subsequent layers, into denser 'firn'. The weight continues to increase, and the firn becomes even more solid. The escalating pressure squeezes air from between the flakes leaving only a few miniscule bubbles as new and much larger crystals form. Eventually that original powdery snow is transformed into ice – glacial ice – and high in the Antarctic ice sheet our itinerant icebergs are conceived.

Antarctica facts

- At 14,000,000 km² Antarctica is the world's fifth largest continent. It's about 1.3 times bigger than Europe or as large as the US and half of Mexico combined.
- Antarctica divides into East Antarctica and smaller West Antarctica, separated by the Transantarctic Mountains.
- Antarctica contains 90 per cent of the world's ice; that's 70 per cent of the world's water.
- 13,700,000 km², or 29,000,000 km³, of ice covers 98 per cent of the continent.
- The weight of ice depresses the continent more than 1 km into the earth, below sea level in some places.
- 11 per cent of the ice is in ice-shelves.
- If all Antarctica's ice melted the world's oceans would rise 60 m.

The early life of Antarctica

- 190 Mya (million years ago) the ancient super-continent Gondwana came into being. It was made up of the land masses that would eventually become Antarctica, South America, Australia and New Guinea, Africa, India and Arabia and New Zealand. Fossil evidence shows that Antarctica was, at some periods, a warm green continent covered in trees and plants.
- 167–80 Mya Africa and India split off from Gondwana.
- 80–40 Mya Australia and Antarctica split apart and ice began to form on Antarctica.
- 30–23 Mya South America pulled away from Antarctica opening Drake Passage between the two. Before then, cold water from the south had been channelled northwards, and exchanged for warmer tropical currents. When Drake Passage opened, this exchange stopped. Cold circumpolar currents developed and accelerated the spread of ice that replaced the existing forest cover of the southern continent.
- Since 15 Mya Antarctica has largely been covered with ice.
- There have been subsequent periods of relative warmth. Only 125,000 years ago the younger West Antarctic Ice Sheet (WAIS) may have disappeared. It has waxed and waned in thickness since then.
- The world's last glacial period was 20,000 years ago. Antarctica's ice shelves expanded until they reached the edge of the continental shelf about 13,000 years ago and they have slowly retreated since then.

Antarctica's Northern Victoria Land coast with glaciers spilling off the polar plateau. NEVILLE PEAT

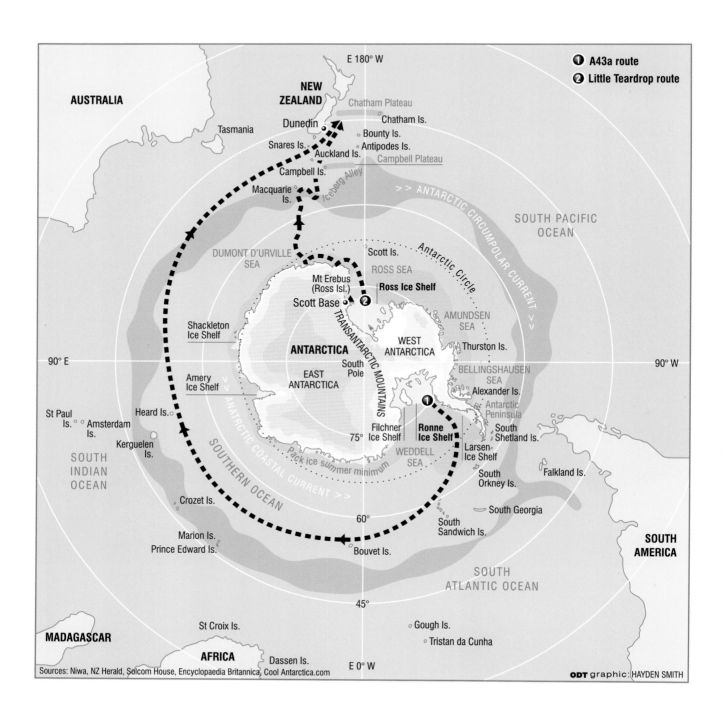

AUSTRALIA

E 180° W

NEW ZEALAND

Chatham Plateau

Tasmania

Dunedin

Chatham Is.

Bounty Is.

Snares Is.

Antipodes Is.

Auckland Is.

Campbell Plateau

Campbell Is.

Iceberg Alley

Macquarie Is.

> > ANTARCTIC CIRCUMPOLAR CURRENT

SOUTH PACIFIC OCEAN

DUMONT D'URVILLE SEA

Scott Is.

Antarctic Circle

ROSS SEA

Mt Erebus (Ross Isl.)

Ross Ice Shelf

AMUNDSEN SEA

Scott Base ❷

Shackleton Ice Shelf

TRANSANTARCTIC MOUNTAINS

WEST ANTARCTICA

Thurston Is.

90° E

ANTARCTICA

South Pole

BELLINGSHAUSEN SEA

90° W

Amery Ice Shelf

EAST ANTARCTICA

Alexander Is.

Antarctic Peninsula

ANTARCTIC COASTAL CURRENT > >

❶

St Paul Is.

Heard Is.

Amsterdam Is.

Pack ice summer minimum

Filchner Ice Shelf

Ronne Ice Shelf

South Shetland Is.

Kerguelen Is.

75°

Larsen Ice Shelf

SOUTH INDIAN OCEAN

SOUTHERN OCEAN

WEDDELL SEA

South Orkney Is.

Falkland Is.

Crozet Is.

South Georgia

Marion Is.

60°

South Sandwich Is.

Prince Edward Is.

SOUTH AMERICA

Bouvet Is.

SOUTH ATLANTIC OCEAN

45°

MADAGASCAR

St Croix Is.

Gough Is.

Tristan da Cunha

AFRICA

Dassen Is.

E 0° W

❶ A43a route
❷ Little Teardrop route

Sources: Niwa, NZ Herald, Solcom House, Encyclopaedia Britannica, Cool Antarctica.com

ODT graphic: HAYDEN SMITH

Pure glacial ice is over 200 times denser than freshly fallen snow and, at its deepest, the Antarctic ice sheet is more than 4 km thick. How much snow had to fall over hundreds of thousands of years to make that much ice?

When over 50 m thick, ice loses much of its brittle nature and becomes more plastic, like very thick toffee – and like toffee it will flow. The pull of gravity on its enormous mass, and the continual build-up from behind, forces the Antarctic ice sheet to spread out in all directions from the giant ice plateau at the centre of the continent. It's rather like pouring thick pancake batter into the middle of a pan. As more is poured on top, the batter oozes towards the edges of the pan.

Much of the sheet grinds along imperceptibly slowly, or is virtually immobile, anchored to rock far below. But between those static ice ridges, massive glacial streams of ice slide over saturated clay sediment. The Antarctic ice sheet counts hundreds of ice streams and glaciers within its constantly morphing mantle. They flow eventually into coastal ice shelves or directly to the edge of the continent.

The embryos of our icebergs started their long journey in one of those glacial streams. It would be a long gestation: some two thousand years, maybe much longer, sliding and grinding their way to the coast.

How glaciers move

Larger ice sheets move by internal deformation. Ice builds up in the centre and forces the edges to expand. Friction between the grinding ice and the rock beneath can melt the bottom ice, allowing the glacier to glide along on the resulting water. In other instances, layers of ice slide over each other. Those layers often have different crystal alignments, and part of the movement of glacial ice is caused by on-going recrystalisation deep in the glacial stream.

The flow speed of the fast outlet glaciers and ice streams embedded in the WAIS depends on a number of factors:
• the weight of ice building up behind
• the steepness of the slope beneath
• ice temperature
• the nature of the rock surface below. Ice will slide over relatively unstable sediments, like saturated clay, more easily than over solid rock.

The West Antarctic Ice Sheet (WAIS) contains about 13 per cent of Antarctica's ice. It is separated from the much larger and older high ice plateau of East Antarctica by the Transantarctic Mountains that run for 3,500 km between the Ross and Weddell seas. One of the longest mountain ranges in the world, the Transantarctic holds back the East Antarctic Ice Sheet (EAIS) like a high dam, but it is penetrated by several glaciers that feed the Ross, Ronne and Filchner ice shelves in the west. WAIS is the world's only marine ice sheet – so named because the bedrock it sits on is below sea level.

Our baby icebergs may initially have been conceived in the WAIS. Or they may have started life somewhere high on East Antarctica's ice plateau and been carried through the mountains in a glacier. No one knows for sure; but we do know they moved through the WAIS, because eventually they flowed into ice shelves, west of the mountains.

❄   ❄   ❄

Ice shelf edge – Antarctica.

Ice shelves

When glacial ice streams and sheets reach the coast, they can't just stop. More ice is pushing from behind. Some glaciers dump hunks of ice directly into the sea as they reach the waterline. But in most areas around Antarctica's shoreline, the ice sheet keeps moving out onto the water and forms an ice shelf. Ice is lighter than water so it floats. The point at which an ice sheet lets go of the land and starts floating is called the 'grounding line'. Above that the ice sheet remains fixed to the land (grounded), so the grounding line is like a hinge, with the floating shelf being lifted up and down by the tides. This could create the impression that an ice shelf is a relatively thin sheet over the water. Not so. Ice shelves range in thickness from 100 m to a staggering 1000 m and can stretch for hundreds of kilometres. They can last for thousands of years.

- An ice shelf is a thick floating platform of ice that forms where a glacier or ice sheet flows down to a coastline and onto the ocean surface.
- Ice shelves cover 50 per cent of Antarctica's coast; that's 10 per cent of the area of the continent.
- Ice shelves differ from sea ice that forms on water and is thinner. Sea ice can hold fast to the land or float free as drift ice (in large quantities: pack ice).
- Ross Ice Shelf, the world's largest, is the size of France and is fed by seven ice streams.
- The 430,000 km² Ronne-Filchner Ice Shelf is the world's second largest, but contains the greatest volume of ice.
- Ice shelves ride the tides, grating against the rocks and eventually breaking apart.
- Ice shelves don't grow forever. Periodically, pieces break off their edges and these are known as icebergs. The birth of an iceberg is called calving.
- Since the last Ice Age, which ended 12,000 years ago, it's thought that the volume of ice lost from ice shelves each year has roughly equalled the amount gained by Antarctica as snowfall. Thus the total amount of moisture on the continent is thought to be in equilibrium.
- Ice shelves can collapse catastrophically. The Larsen B Shelf collapsed in 2002 when more than 720 billion tonnes of ice broke up into the sea in little over a month. Larsen B had existed since the last Ice Age. Scientists are still debating the causes, but a combination of warmer air and seawater is thought to be responsible.

The Ross Ice Shelf, the size of France, extends a long way beyond Scott Base. The American ice-shelf runway, Williams Field, can be seen in the distance in this January 2007 view. NEVILLE PEAT

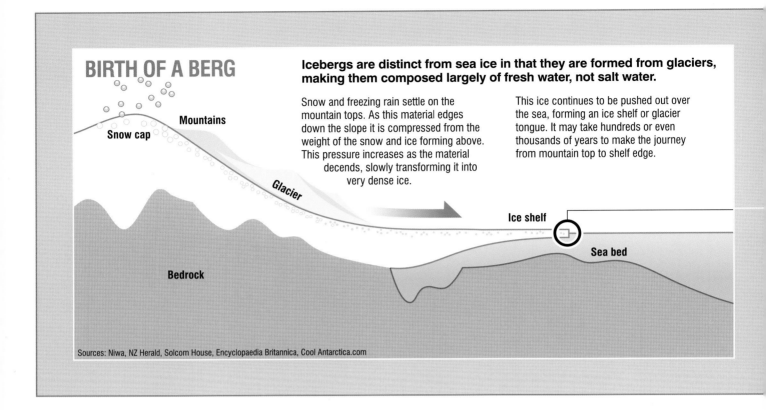

BIRTH OF A BERG

Icebergs are distinct from sea ice in that they are formed from glaciers, making them composed largely of fresh water, not salt water.

Snow and freezing rain settle on the mountain tops. As this material edges down the slope it is compressed from the weight of the snow and ice forming above. This pressure increases as the material decends, slowly transforming it into very dense ice.

This ice continues to be pushed out over the sea, forming an ice shelf or glacier tongue. It may take hundreds or even thousands of years to make the journey from mountain top to shelf edge.

Mountains

Snow cap

Glacier

Ice shelf

Sea bed

Bedrock

Sources: Niwa, NZ Herald, Solcom House, Encyclopaedia Britannica, Cool Antarctica.com

So after thousands of years of gestation, and another two millennia inching through the WAIS, our embryonic icebergs finally approach their birthplace: the icebound Antarctic coast.

On reaching a coastal ice shelf, ice has to queue up. Eons of earlier ice forms the shelf ahead, but as that ice pushes out to sea, our potential bergs are jostled further and further from land. Here they experience the first forces of disintegration: the sea below is warmer than ice, and can melt the base of the ice shelf; and the air above sometimes rises to a point where surface melting occurs.

However both these melting effects may be counteracted. Snow inevitably builds up on

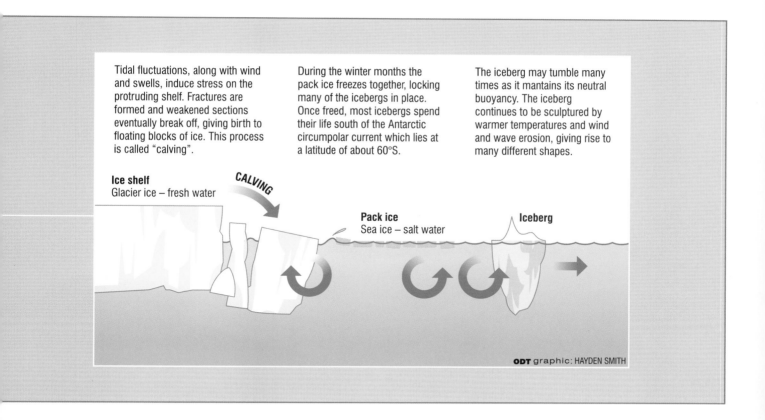

Tidal fluctuations, along with wind and swells, induce stress on the protruding shelf. Fractures are formed and weakened sections eventually break off, giving birth to floating blocks of ice. This process is called "calving".

During the winter months the pack ice freezes together, locking many of the icebergs in place. Once freed, most icebergs spend their life south of the Antarctic circumpolar current which lies at a latitude of about 60°S.

The iceberg may tumble many times as it maintains its neutral buoyancy. The iceberg continues to be sculptured by warmer temperatures and wind and wave erosion, giving rise to many different shapes.

Ice shelf
Glacier ice – fresh water

CALVING

Pack ice
Sea ice – salt water

Iceberg

ODT graphic: HAYDEN SMITH

the ice sheet surface, sometimes several metres deep. As the snow packs down to firn, the shelf thickness increases. However on the base something less predictable can happen: high saline, super-cooled seawater can freeze to the underside of the shelf. Using hot water drills, scientists have discovered that the bottom 80 m of the Ronne Ice Shelf is sometimes frozen seawater called marine ice. So over many years, as the ice within the shelf is pushed relentlessly out from the grounding line, it develops three layers: the firn layer on top, the ancient glacial ice in the middle making up the bulk of the shelf, and frozen sea water on the bottom.

Ice shelves don't keep growing forever, and while they lose mass through melting on top or underneath, by far the most significant reduction to their volume is through calving icebergs. Quite simply, and for a variety of reasons, chunks of ice shelf periodically break off. The icebergs can be enormous: hundreds of kilometres long – the size of a small European country, or an American state.

Why do they break off? Usually because melting of the base leaves insufficient ice below the waterline to support the weight of ice above. In other words, a portion of the shelf has become top heavy.

Just as influential in creating icebergs are tides and storms. As a shelf grows further from its

Dwarfed by its quarry, a sightseeing helicopter circles a wave-weathered berg.

grounding line, movement and flexing increases and exacerbates inevitable weaknesses in the shelf itself. Top crevasses can fill with melt water, forcing the crevasses to open wider as they work their way down. Bottom crevasses, over 100 m wide and deep, reach up from the base of the sheet. Such rifts may not penetrate the entire shelf thickness, but they can create a weakness or 'break line', like a perforation in a sheet of paper. The next big storm, or spring tide, is the final straw, and the shelf breaks along a crevasse, losing a piece of itself into the ocean.

Calving events can be extraordinarily spectacular and are often, not surprisingly, accompanied by a distinctive loud crack. An ice shelf may rise 100 m above the ocean surface. When even a relatively small (by Antarctic standards) iceberg 'calves' and plunges into the sea, it can cause a minor tsunami. Anything other than a large ship would be swamped. In many cases however, the birth of an iceberg, especially a very large one, would be most noticeable (if anyone were actually present to watch) many kilometres from the edge of the ice shelf. Large cracks, both top and bottom, work their way through the ice and gradually lengthen over many years. Eventually the stresses of tide and storm, the constant flexing and the stupendous weight of the overhanging shelf prove too much. The crack becomes an irreparable breach, ripping open like a long zipper, and a new-born ice monster floats free.

There are at least two dozen significant ice shelves around Antarctica. Which one was the birthplace of our icebergs? As it would turn out, they had drifted off and melted away somewhere north-east of Christchurch before we knew for certain exactly where in Antarctica they had calved.

There are obviously many possible areas of origin. But these were soon narrowed down to just two. NIWA (New Zealand's National Institute of Water and Atmospheric Research) scientists believed the parent iceberg originated from the Ronne Ice Shelf, the western and larger side of the Ronne-Filchner Ice Shelf. The iceberg they had in mind was known as A43.

Other evidence pointed to the vast Ross Ice Shelf, on the other side of West Antarctica as the origin. The B15 family of icebergs, plus others that calved around the same time, were the suspects here. B15 and A43 calved in the same year: 2000. That much they had in common. But where, along the 18,000 km Antarctica coastline, the parent berg calved makes a huge difference to the sea route it would have to take to reach New Zealand.

❋   ❋   ❋

How icebergs are named

Whenever a new iceberg is noticed, it is given a name by the US National Ice Center. The first part is a letter, A, B, C or D, and denotes the Antarctic quadrant in which it was first sighted. It also has a sequential number. Whenever an iceberg breaks up, each new berg that measures over ten nautical miles in length, has an additional letter added to its original number. So when A43 broke up, the resulting bergs were named A43a, A43b and so on.

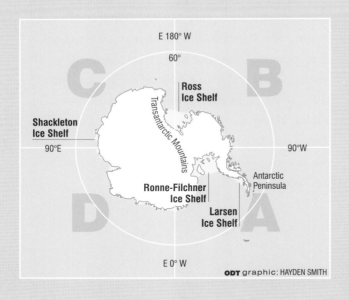

Reconnoitring a boulder field on a drydock berg.

A typically tabular Antarctic iceberg.

Arctic calling

Scientists endeavouring to identify the causes of iceberg calving have made a startling discovery. Ocean swells generated by storms in the Arctic, literally on the other side of the planet, may instigate calving of the Antarctic ice shelves. In one instance it was found that ocean swells from a storm in the Gulf of Alaska arrived at Antarctica six days later, immediately prior to and during the calving of a huge iceberg from Cape Adare.

A43 – From the other side of the world

On 5 May 2000 two large icebergs, A43 and A44, calved from the western edge of the Ronne Ice Shelf. A43 was 34 km wide and 250 km long. Two days later she split to form A43a and A43b, the former still 5544 km² in area. That's nearly two and-a-half times the size of Stewart Island. A43a would break up many more times during the next six years, creating hundreds of icebergs.

It's a long way from the Ronne Ice Shelf to New Zealand's South Island. It is literally the other side of the world. Even as the crow flies it's nearly 6000 km. A43a couldn't fly direct, so it is speculated that she took the much more circuitous route north from the Weddell Sea, and then eastwards, almost three quarters of the way around Antarctica to New Zealand; a total journey of nearly 14,000 km. Why would she follow that route?

For three and a half years A43a stayed close to her birthplace in the Weddell Sea. Pack ice, particularly during the winters, constrained her movement. Then she gradually drifted north towards South Georgia, and was last seen officially on 30 January 2005 in the Scotia Sea. That is right in the path of the world's longest ocean current, the Antarctic Circumpolar Current (ACC). Even the monster A43a could not resist that, and she was propelled inexorably eastward.

The Antarctic Circumpolar Current

This 21,000 km current, also known as the West Wind Drift, flows continually eastwards around the world between latitudes 50° and 60° South. Driven by relentless westerly winds, it carries more than 100 times the flow of all the world's rivers combined. At its most constricted point, Drake Passage, between South America and the Antarctic Peninsula, the Current's flow is about 134,000,000 m³ per second.

The ACC is made possible by the unique geography of the Southern Ocean, which isn't defined or surrounded by landmasses. Instead it surrounds a landmass, the Antarctic, while along its northern boundary, known as the Antarctic Convergence, it blends into the Atlantic, Pacific and Indian oceans. The Southern Ocean is the only part of the planet in which you can sail around the world in a straight line without making landfall. Therefore there are no obstacles to the Current's continuous circling.

✳ ✳ ✳

From the time A43a departed the Scotia Sea and drifted up past South Georgia, she would have about 20 months to reach the seas south of New Zealand. That's a journey of some 13,500 kms at an average speed of around 21.5 km per day. The maximum speed of the Antarctic Circumpolar Current (ACC) is around 7 kph, so if A43a made the trip it's likely she took a northern track where the Current is closer to the surface. Icebergs move at the whim of ocean currents, not wind, and 90 per cent of their volume is beneath the sea surface. With so much ballast below, even the ferocious winds of the Southern Ocean barely stir them. As icebergs become smaller, wind and wave action have more effect. However the farther north A43a drifted, the warmer the waters, and the more likely she was to melt and break up, perhaps before reaching New Zealand.

Certainly during her long journey, A43a would have broken into smaller pieces. When last spotted on 30 January 2005 in the Scotia Sea, she was estimated at 51 km long and 21 km wide. That is about 360 times bigger than the largest berg spotted by the New Zealand Air Force on 4 November 2006.

The process of disintegration is incessant. In addition to repeated splitting, wind, rain and sun melt the exposed upper surface, while relatively warmer seawater erodes the vast base. Because of that, A43a's descendants would look nothing like their venerable ancestor: different shapes and sizes entirely. So how can we tell if they are our passing bergs?

On a return flight from the bergs, Southern Lakes Helicopters pilot Richard Hayes climbs to 3000 m as he approaches Otago Peninsula.

Pack ice and icebergs in the Ross Sea. They look like confetti, but some of the bergs are kilometres across. NEVILLE PEAT

B15 – a local iceberg from a local source?

B15 was first discovered on 17 March 2000. She had just calved from the eastern portion of the Ross Ice Shelf. At 295 km long by 37 km wide – that's larger than Jamaica – B15 may have been the largest iceberg ever observed. Even when she split in two in May 2000, the resulting B15a still covered 3100 km², and was the largest free-floating object on the planet. Over the next five years, B15a caused mayhem in the Ross Sea.

From the years 2000 to 2003 B15a didn't move far but pieces continued to break off into smaller bergs. Then in 2003 she drifted away from Ross Island and eventually into McMurdo Sound where she parked and stayed for nearly two years. McMurdo Sound is home to New Zealand's Scott Base, McMurdo Base (USA) and large colonies of penguins, particularly Adelies. All three were drastically affected by the behemoth B15a overstaying her welcome.

Most summers, ocean and wind currents break up the Sound's sea ice. But during the summer of 2004–05, B15a's enormous presence blocked those currents off, protecting and preserving the sea ice. Shipping access to the two polar stations

29

was drastically curtailed and the penguins suffered even more. Deprived of easy access to open waters for feeding, the adult Adelies had to walk many kilometres for food and then the same distance back to feed their young. The colonies were decimated, and many penguins died.

Finally in the autumn of 2005, B15a was on the move again, and heading for more trouble. She was drifting directly towards the Drygalski Ice Tongue. The 70 km-long Tongue is the floating outflow of the David Glacier. Floating ice it may be, but since it's discovery by Robert Falcon Scott during his 1901–03 expedition, it's been a permanent feature on Antarctica's maps. B15a, still 122 km by 28 km, looked set to amend local geography with one king hit. Then just 5 km from the Tongue she stalled, grounded on the shallow shoals that have presumably protected the Drygalski from just such collisions for thousands of years. Gradually B15a swung around and broke free and, on a different track, she edged past Drygalski delivering only a glancing blow. That was sufficient however to break a 5 km-long chunk from Drygalski's tip.

B15a sailed on to menace the Aviator Glacier Ice Tongue, but this time there was no damage, and B15a drifted north. By October 2005 she was aground off Cape Adare where she broke up into nine long 'knife-shaped' icebergs. These, the remainder of the B15 family, eventually broke free of the sea ice that was hemming them in, and drifted westwards close to the Antarctica shoreline.

This is the typical path for icebergs originating in the Ross Sea, as they are picked up by the

Antarctic Coastal Current

Also known as the Antarctic Polar Current and the East Wind Drift, the Antarctic Coastal Current flows anti-clockwise close to the Antarctic coast, driven by easterly polar winds. Its flow around Antarctica is not complete, however. The Antarctic Peninsula obstructs it and in Drake Passage, between the Peninsula and South America, it can't compete with the clockwise flowing Antarctic Circumpolar Current – at that point, one of the strongest currents on earth. As a result, the Coastal Current turns back on itself in several gyres.

anti-clockwise Antarctic Coastal Current. Edging north though, they would eventually be caught by the irresistible Antarctic Circumpolar Current flowing in the opposite direction, and propelled east and maybe north. Was B15 the ancestor of our visiting bergs?

❄   ❄   ❄

Adelie penguin breeding colony. LLOYD SPENCER DAVIS

Floating ice cliffs – Antarctica. © D GIVEN, ANTARCTICA NZ PICTORIAL COLLECTION RSRSOER

Rivulets of ice-melt gash an iceberg's surface.

Arctic versus Antarctic icebergs

Icebergs also calve from glaciers in Greenland and Alaska. However there are two major differences between Northern and Southern Hemisphere icebergs:

- Most northern icebergs calve directly into the sea from parent glaciers, while Antarctic bergs usually calve from ice shelves. This gives the bergs a different shape. Antarctic bergs tend to be large and flat-topped (tabular). Northern bergs are smaller and more compact.
- Greenland icebergs tend to be composed entirely of fresh-water glacial ice. Antarctic icebergs have an upper layer of permeable firn, and sometimes have a bottom layer of frozen seawater.

33

Icebergs clearly visible from Dunedin's high points.
PETER MCINTOSH/*ODT*

Unexpected visitors

It was inevitable that both groups of icebergs, the descendants of B15 and A43, would end up in the grip of the Antarctic Circumpolar Current. As it approaches the area south of New Zealand, the Current collides with the extensive submarine Campbell Plateau, and is either forced south around it, or temporarily breaks up into giant eddies, before reforming and continuing eastwards. If the A43a armada had got this far, their course somewhat north of the usual iceberg highway may have directed them between the Auckland Islands and Stewart Island, rather than south of the Aucklands. So instead of veering south at the Campbell Plateau, it is proposed that some of the A43a armada caught an eddy and were pushed into the Southland Current that runs up the east coast of the South Island before flowing out east towards the Chatham Islands. B15a and kin may have been grabbed by the same eddying currents.

We didn't expect them. We knew that dozens, even hundreds of bergs were floating past the Auckland Islands, but expert opinion was unanimous: 'They won't come north and they certainly won't come anywhere near the New Zealand mainland.'

Photographers from around the world came to view the icebergs.
PETER MCINTOSH/ODT

❅　❅　❅

Hundreds of sightseers flew out in fixed-wing planes and helicopters for a close-up iceberg experience.

But they did, and were among the most celebrated visitors Otago has hosted in years. News and television crews from further north and even Australia descended on Dunedin, and night after night regaled viewers with images from another world, right on our doorstep. Several news crews and individuals actually landed on some of the bergs, planting a variety of flags as transient testimony to their nerve. Even celebrity merino, Shrek, replete with custom-made crampons and a giant wool hanging, took a bow as he was shorn atop a flat berg. Up close, the floating islands were a source of surprise, wonderment, and not a little apprehension.

On several days, the bergs were visible on the horizon from Dunedin's higher vantage points, where a variety of binoculars, telescopes and telephoto lenses willed them closer. Apparently that wasn't close enough for some of the more adventurous. Rumour has it that some thrill-seeking souls boated out and dived around a berg, and when it rolled they were lucky to escape unscathed. Or was that an urban myth spawned by the icebergs' mystique?

❄ ❄ ❄

Left: Ice deltas wrought by wind and wave presage the disintegration of an iceberg.

Demand was such that Richard Hayes made several long chopper flights from Te Anau to ferry news crews out to the bergs.

It was dubbed 'the harbour' by pilots, but this drydock iceberg would not have offered safe mooring.

All shapes and sizes

Sizes:

- Brash ice — from ice cube to base ball size
- Growlers — 1 m to 3 m across. Sailors often hear a growling sound as these bob in the water
- Bergy bits — up to 5 m high and 15 m long
- Bergs — higher than 5 m
- Tabular bergs or ice islands — the colossi of the iceberg world. Plates of ice up to 1 km thick.

Shapes:

- Tabular — steep sides with long flat top
- Blocky — similar to tabular but smaller top relative to height
- Dome — small with a rounded top
- Wedge — one flat side slopes gradually to the water. The opposite side slopes steeply. The two sides meet at the peak as a spine
- Pinnacle — one or more sharp peaks
- Drydock — two or more peaks separated by a water-filled channel.

Most Antarctic icebergs start out in tabular form. The statuesque peaks and crenellations of Pinnacle and Drydock bergs are probably not a result of top surface melting. Rather, as the warmer seawater erodes the base, the iceberg becomes unbalanced and eventually tips over. That exposes the exotic carving wrought by the sea.

The Australian Channel 9 TV crew had to be especially vigilant. Descending in the helicopter towards the iceberg, they had watched a rogue wave wash up as far as the lake.

Iceberg colours

Most icebergs are white because of their covering of snow or bubble-filled ice. However many icebergs appear to be dark blue-green or cyan; but if a small piece of ice is removed, it is clear. That's because thick, bubble-free ice absorbs only a small portion of the red light entering it, so appears blue. Occasionally icebergs come in other colours. Green bergs are the result of algae which is growing in marine (sea) ice below the waterline and is only seen when the berg tips over. Some bergs appear almost black, or have clearly defined chocolate stripes. This is caused by mineral impurities or moraine debris picked up by glacial base ice in contact with rock, soil or sand.

This imposing conning-tower of ice succumbed to the sea soon after this photograph was taken.

Quite accustomed to car travel, Shrek arrived at Taieri Airfield sporting 2.5 years of wool growth.

Shrek

Shrek is a Merino wether (castrated male sheep) who catapulted into national celebrity when he was discovered during the 2004 muster (round-up) on Bendigo Station, a Central Otago hill country sheep ranch. The nine-year-old hermit's ear tag proved he had been avoiding capture in the desiccated hills, 1500 m above sea level, for six years. His 38 cm long, bulky, matted fleece covered his face and made him almost unrecognisable. He was subsequently relieved of the 27 kg coat on prime-time television.

His owner, John Perriam, saw Shrek's earning potential and the popular ovine has subsequently raised over $100,000 for the charity Cure Kids.

Shrek was named by local children, who reckoned that like the film character, his ogreish appearance hid a gentle spirit. So it has proved. Whether mixing with large crowds or meeting the Prime Minister, Shrek maintains a dignified, friendly demeanour.

The nearest settlement to Bendigo is Tarras. Its school's thirteen children wrote a book about Shrek with locally produced illustrations. So far, over 30,000 copies have been sold — proceeds go to the school. Shrek's iceberg excursion was the entrepreneurial wether's first off-shore charity event.

Shrek with owner John Perriam en route by helicopter to the icebergs. PETER MCINTOSH/*ODT*

John Perriam — farmer and owner of Shrek

'It was like trying to stand on a curling rink. When Shrek realized how slippery it was he just went down like a big seal.

'Standing there makes you realize the scale and power of nature. It was a vast piece of ice with sheer drops to the sea below. I don't think the immersion suits [for buoyancy and insulation] would have made much difference [if we had fallen in].

'On the way out to the bergs the pilots had been talking about a storm coming up from

Walking and working on a surface as slippery as wet glass, humans as well as Shrek wore crampons for safety.
PETER MCINTOSH/*ODT*

Shrek's made-to-order crampons. PETER MCINTOSH/*ODT*

the south. So there was a bit of anxiety to get things done quickly and get off. When I heard lightning and thunder I looked up at the sky, but then I realized the rumbling was all happening underneath us. The whole iceberg started quivering. There were big cracks ripping through it and you couldn't help wondering which one would swallow us up.

'But then a big piece fell off. After that it was calm and we just got on with the job. Shrek was pretty good, and Jimmy Barnett [shearer] was very laid back. He didn't get fazed even though it was tough shearing two years' growth with blades.'

Shearer Jimmy Barnett, John Perriam and Shrek arrive on the iceberg. PETER MCINTOSH/ODT

An 'all-wether' sheep; Shrek sits untethered beside camera equipment as preparations for shearing are made. PETER MCINTOSH/*ODT*

Where there's a wool there's a way. Shrek being shorn. PETER MCINTOSH/*ODT*

A job well done.

Deep cracks foreshadow the next ice cube into the drink.

What a difference a day makes. Having shed tonnes of its bulk in just 24 hours,
the now lighter and smaller iceberg rides much higher in water.

TV3 reporter Mark Price dressed in a protective suit worn by all media visitors.

Sea ice expert Dr Pat Langhorne became a familiar face through her role as media commentator.

Mark Price – TV3 reporter

'I had thought we would find just great flat boring hunks of ice, but we lucked on the first iceberg with the big tower. It will always stay in my mind: that huge column of ice sticking up. It was the most brilliant sight.

'When I hit the ice I expected it to be unstable somehow: like being on a boat, and there was a good swell. But it was like being on the land. It was so solid, so stable. It was really like being on an island.

'While we were doing the standup [spoken piece to camera], I could hear these rifle-shot sounds. Real sharp cracks ringing out. I honestly thought it was a gun being fired. It turned out to be the ice cracking.

'It was absolutely spectacular out there, so pristine: clean, bright and white. There was no sign of footprints, no dirt, no rocks, no animals, no people; just amazing.'

Mere dots on an icy slope, veteran newsmen from Australian Channel 9's 'A Current Affair' programme, described their iceberg reports as among the top stories of their careers.

Apprehension written all over his face, Australian Channel 9 reporter Ben McCormack leads his camera crew Tim Hawkins and Scott Pritchard back to the security of the chopper.

Stephen Jaquiery – *Otago Daily Times* photographer

'I had no idea what we were going to find, or what shape the iceberg would be. Whether it would be a smooth flat surface or covered in ice boulders or what. We opened the door and found this big, boulder field of ice. The ice boulders all had these iridescent blue shadows under them. Beautiful. No black shadows, and the cliff face was pouring with water.

'It was a bit like stepping out onto the moon. You didn't really know what was going to happen when you put your foot down. The surface, apart from where the boulders were, was shiny and wet, like wet glass. I didn't feel secure.

'Another time, when we were out shearing Shrek, it was on a large flat iceberg. We were just getting the mat organised, when we heard a rippling, crackling sound from some distance away, coming directly towards us. You could imagine that the whole iceberg was breaking up. It came towards us and went under our feet. That was most unsettling. I immediately called up the helicopter and said "Come back here please and make sure this iceberg isn't breaking in half."

Self-portrait of a news photographer.

Left: Setting up for shearing. PETER MCINTOSH/ODT

Stephen Jaquiery and Shrek with the offending waratah and ODT flag.
JOHN PERRIAM

'Fortunately they could see what had happened. A big lump of the iceberg had broken off the other side and fallen into the sea.

'I found out later on that the structure of the ice in an iceberg is like glass, and if you put a little mark in it, potentially it can break. In fact John Perriam had been told by some scientists that we shouldn't even wear crampons.

'I didn't know that at the time, and when John was gathering all the wool together, he was horrified to hear this clonk, clonk, clonk in the background. It was me, banging a waratah into the ice to fly the ODT flag! The pilots told us, when they went out the next day, that the part of the iceberg we were standing on had disappeared.

'It was extraordinarily exciting going out and landing and walking around on the icebergs, but it was an even greater relief getting off them.'

The first iceberg seen in Otago waters leads the way. The ice tower is over 100 m high.

This twin engine BK helicopter flew sightseeing trips out to the icebergs every two hours
during daylight, but still could not keep up with demand.

Damon Forde – TV3 cameraman

'I used to work in search and rescue, so I was aware of what could go wrong. So I just wanted to get everything we had to do, done, and get out of there, because I knew the potential for disaster was quite high really: breaking up, bits falling down. We could hear it creaking. There was also an incredible amount of water flowing down the sides, so you knew it was melting fast. The bergs are just waiting to tip over and break up by the time they get here.

'They were bigger than I anticipated, and harder to shoot, because as you go round them, the light is changing the whole time. They are really bright. But our pics were better than the opposition because we had a nice, bright, sunny day and a dark sea. That made the bergs stand out more.

'It's quite an odd sensation standing on them. Parts were almost transparent but blue beneath. It looks like there's only 50 mm of ice then water. You know that the ice is thick but it's a very odd feeling stepping off the chopper skid for the first time. I was standing on the ice still harnessed to the helicopter and thinking "I don't really want to unclip this thing".'

❄ ❄ ❄

The visiting icebergs entranced us, and fired our imaginations. One romantically inclined couple wanted to put their love on ice by celebrating their nuptials on a berg. Sadly for them, being outside New Zealand territorial waters and without a designated captain on board 'ship', the icebergs, for all their solidity, were deemed legally non-existent. Another pair, meeting by chance in a sightseeing helicopter, exchanged seats for better views, then glances, then marriage vows some three months later.

People came from as far away as Australia especially to see our icebergs, all for slightly different reasons. One sightseer had lost a son who had worked in Antarctica, and she wanted to see the ice that had come from the south. Hundreds of sightseers viewed the icebergs from helicopters and fixed-wing planes. In fact the sheer volume of air traffic posed some risks.

Five metre swells dwarfed by an eroding iceberg.

The shearing team and Shrek on the stern, give scale to this 'aircraft carrier' berg. PETER MCINTOSH/ODT

Right: Like a sleeping shark, this berg looks docile
and secure, but appearances can be deceptive.

Fly-in: two Southern Lakes choppers and a Helicopters Otago in the background.

John Penno – Chief Flying Instructor – Mainland Air

'We only took twin engine planes out as we liked the idea of getting home.

'We worked with Graeme Gale [Helicopters Otago Ltd] to keep the risks down. We had a good team thing going. We'd fly at 600 feet and he'd fly at 400 feet. So we knew there was separation. But the biggest risks were from private pilots. Some people flew out in incredibly lightweight planes: homebuilts etc. Crazy. One guy in a single-engined plane flew so close past the iceberg that the oscillations off his prop hit the water and splashed his plane. I got on the phone to the idiot and told him to leave his f....... aircraft in the hangar.'

John Penno, chief pilot for Mainland Air.

❆   ❆   ❆

But even the most safety conscious of professionals copped their share of criticism.

Graeme Gale – Helicopters Otago Ltd

'I came under criticism that I shouldn't be landing on them. Well Sir Edmund Hillary's mother probably told him not to walk up Mt Everest. Get a life. Safety is paramount for us, but we are Kiwis. We are adventurers.

'It got reported that we were landing with passengers but we didn't go down and let any passengers out at all. But we did for the media and for research. But you had to pick your spot and be very careful.

'I'd never seen an iceberg before, not even around Auckland Islands and Campbell Island and we go down there on a regular basis for rescue work.

'They were extremely impressive. Pretty awesome. I haven't seen any photos that show you how really amazing they were. The colours were always changing. The light was changing. Everything was moving all the time.

'You'd go out in the morning and find the light completely different from the evening before. The icebergs had changed. It might have rolled. Bits might have broken off. It looks like a totally different iceberg. Every flight was different. People always wanted to go to the biggest iceberg, but it didn't matter whether you went to the smallest or the largest, they all still looked fantastic. The shapes, the colours, they were all absolutely fantastic.'

Pilots soon learned to respect these soaring towers for the turbulent airflow they caused.

Sea ice sanctuary. An Adelie penguin jumps aboard. LLOYD SPENCER DAVIS

The Southern Ocean

In those six-and-a-half years of drifting, what company did B15a and A43a and their whanau keep? The great Southern Ocean is anything but empty. In the immediate environs of Antarctica there is abundant wildlife. Penguins – Adelie, Emperor, Gentoo and Chinstrap – venture out from land or pack ice to feed. Seals too would pass our icebergs on foraging expeditions – Crabeater, Fur and Weddell – looking for krill and small fish, aggressive Leopard seals hunting the young of other seals and penguins. Overhead the sky would rarely be empty of seabirds: albatrosses, fulmars, gulls, petrels and terns soaring on westerly gales.

Various sub-Antarctic islands further north are home to seven more species of penguins, who would cast a passing glance at our icebergs and even frolic around them as they drifted near land.

The most dramatic passing wildlife traffic however is cetacean. In summer the majestic blue whale, the largest animal ever to live on earth, gorges on krill at the fringes of the ice pack. Southern right, sperm and minke whales also migrate south during summer to breed and feed. The world's largest population of orcas lives around Antarctica, where they hunt and eat pretty much anything they can catch: squid, fish, sharks, penguins and other birds, seals and even the young of other whale species.

All that prolific wildlife attracted the attention of humans. Sealers and whalers were among the first people to venture to the southern continent. The sealers have since disappeared, but Japanese whalers still pursue their lethal 'research', and illegal tooth-fish fishing is rife. Their opponents, protesters like Greenpeace and Sea Shepherd, and fishery protection and naval vessels from several nations increasingly make their presence felt.

A43a and B15a and their fragmented offspring may even have passed the occasional cruise ship en route south.

❄ ❄ ❄

The Southern Ocean is one of the least hospitable areas of ocean on earth. The winds south of the 40° latitude are the strongest, on average, anywhere on the planet. Sailors have long known this. In addition to the Roaring Forties, they coined the phrases Furious Fifties and Screaming Sixties. Remote the area may be, and little traversed except by hardy yachties and fishing boats, but the Southern Ocean is not untouched by human contagion, if only because it abuts the much more frequented Atlantic, Pacific and Indian Oceans. Our icebergs would pass enduring flotsam like plastic bags and bottles, lost shipping containers and slicks of bilge oil. Even more sobering are the mute, bedraggled corpses of petrels and albatrosses, drowned after being hooked on fishermen's long-lines. World Wildlife Fund studies conclude that 40,000 birds are killed this way in the Southern Ocean each year.

Icebergs, the pure crystalline essence of millions of years of polar precipitation, drift on, while all around, the detritus of just a few decades of human exploitation grows ever more conspicuous, and deadly.

❄   ❄   ❄

At 1 km long, this was the largest iceberg to float by the Otago coast.

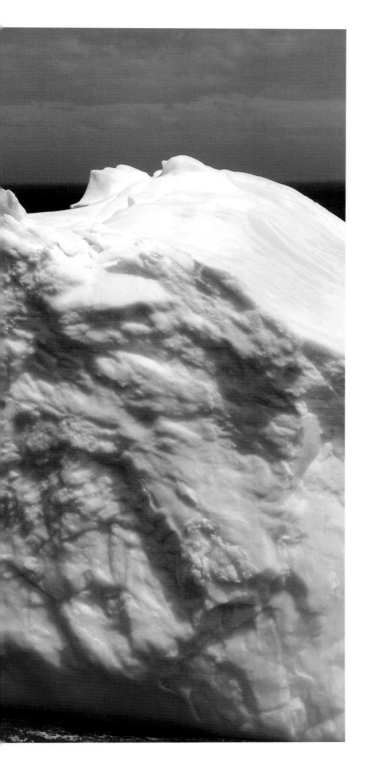

Are our icebergs a sign of global warming?

Apparently if all Antarctic's ice melted the world's oceans would rise by 60 m. So naturally we become apprehensive when we see multiple calvings of large icebergs and the collapse of extensive ice shelves. However, scientists tend to agree that these events are quite different in character, and are probably triggered by different causes. Heightened sea and air temperatures are certainly being observed around the Antarctic Peninsula, and these are possibly a factor in the collapse of the Larsen Shelves on the Peninsula's eastern side. But the Peninsula juts considerably further to the north than the rest of the continent, so may not be a reliable indicator for the whole land mass.

That said, if warming were to accelerate ice melting, the relatively more temperate areas of the region are where you would expect it to start. The jury is still out. Scientists are not even sure that increasing temperatures might not create more ice in the long run rather than less. As temperatures go up, so does condensation, resulting in more snow falling inland, and that turns eventually into more ice.

A combination satellite image shows marine glaciers retreating on the Antarctic Peninsula (top is 1986, lower 2001). A study using aerial photos spanning the last 50 years, found 87 per cent of the 244 marine glaciers on the west side of the Antarctic Peninsula in retreat and the melting rate accelerating. REUTERS

Growlers and bergy bits, the detritus of disintegration, float around their parent iceberg.

Ice shelves retreat and advance by calving, and have done so for thousands of years. Sometimes the areas of shelf lost are stupendous. But that has to be seen over a time scale of millennia, rather than the mere century that humans have been present to observe the process.

However the Antarctic is enormously important to the planet's weather patterns. If things change there, we will all be affected.

❅   ❅   ❅

An iridescent blue lake on a floating crystalline bed.

And where *did* they come from?

Eventually the mystery birthplace of our icebergs was pinpointed. Their parent wasn't A43a from the Ronne Ice Shelf. And it wasn't B15. But it was from the Ross Shelf. In fact the relatively small iceberg that proved to be the progenitor of our armada of bergs, calved right next to, and at the same time as B15. Dubbed 'Little Teardrop' because of her shape, she was never given an official name. The US National Ice Center size-criterion for designating bergs and maintaining data on their size and position is over 10 nautical miles long. Just over 8 nautical miles from nose to tail when she drifted past Macquarie Island, Little Teardrop literally slipped 'under the radar' into our waters.

Little Teardrop calved near Roosevelt Island in March 2000 with the B15 family of icebergs. After drifting northwest with the B15 group, she rounded Cape Adare and then grounded in Rennick Bay in July 2001. About August 2004, she floated free and drifted along the Oates Coast past Mawson Peninsula. By February 2005 she became trapped with C19a and a number of the B bergs, in the 'iceberg graveyard' off Cape Freshfield. However she somehow emerged

in August of that year and drifted north, past C19a and into pack ice. Again Little Teardrop broke free, and in May 2006 she started a rapid ramble north towards New Zealand. All the while of course, she was being pared down by the elements. Then in early October 2006, Little Teardrop split up and lost her distinctive shape. The majestic ice leviathans that hove into view off Otago in November 2006 were her offspring.

Little Teardrop's life story is fascinating enough. But the saga of her discovery and identification is quite extraordinary. By mid November 2006, NIWA had concluded that A43a was the probable ancestor of the visiting icebergs. This was apparently supported by evidence based on isotope analysis of ice core samples taken from the bergs. So the Ronne Ice Shelf became generally accepted as the birthplace.

Then on 15 December 2006, Australia's Antarctic Climate and Ecosystems Cooperative Research Centre posted an article on its website, flatly contradicting that view, and identifying a small iceberg that had calved with the B15 family, as our visitors' ancestor. They didn't give her a name. The Australians turned out to be

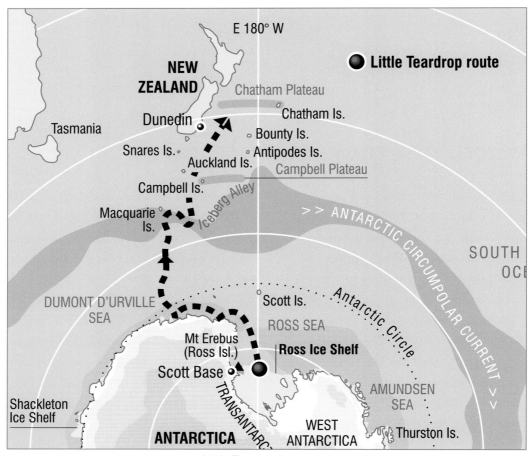

Little Teardrop's journey.

correct. But over a month before they issued their statement, a completely independent, amateur researcher had reached the same conclusion. Christchurch teacher, John Dunbier, unconvinced by the Ronne theory, had launched his own investigation. John reckoned that rather than starting with a known iceberg, and hypothesizing how it might have reached our shores, it would be safer to follow the actual bergs back in

time to find out where they came from. And he found just the mechanism to do that. John went onto NASA's Modis (Moderate Resolution Spectroradiometer) website and searched for photographs of the visiting bergs taken by the cameras on Modis's two satellites: Aqua and Terra.

These satellites achieve daily global coverage at a resolution of up to 250 m. Two images are posted daily at near 'real-time'. Once John had found the bergs, he 'rewound the movie' as he says. He simply went back day-by-day through the Modis archives and followed the small icebergs back in time. Gradually over preceding days, smaller fragments coalesced into larger ones. The flotilla became smaller and more compact and John began to recognize the shapes of small icebergs. By 4 October they had merged as one moderate sized iceberg in the process of splitting. John had found Little Teardrop. She was named by a two- and a-half-year-old girl called Bonni, who reckoned her shape, when minus one 'tail', was that of a teardrop. That distinctive outline made John's job much easier from then on. But then he ran into the murk of the southern winter. For two months prior to mid-July the Modis satellite cameras could see nothing.

Painstakingly trawling back in time, John found his quarry again in an image from 10 May. Her core was the same size and shape, though her 'tails', fore and aft, were fuller and longer. John was pretty sure of his identification, but he had lost her for a full two months. There was a remote, outside chance this was not Little Teardrop.

How to penetrate the sub-Antarctic gloom of June and July and be absolutely certain? What could see in the dark? The answer was obvious: radar! John used another satellite tracking system: radar based QuikSCAT. It's not usually QuikSCAT's job to track icebergs. It is designed to monitor waves and weather, but fortuitously QuikSCAT did image Little Teardrop intermittently through those two black months.

Before and after!

Day 112 (22/4/2006) (before winter). Day 230 (18/8/2006) (after winter).

Images courtesy of MODIS Rapid Response Project at NASA/GSFC

From then on John's tracking became simpler, all the way back through the vicissitudes of Little Teardrop's Antarctic trek, to her calving from the Ross Ice Shelf in March 2000. He even identified her outline as she lay silent in her icy womb just prior to breaking free. The genesis of Little Teardrop's odyssey marked the conclusion of John's.

He last spotted Little Teardrop's progeny out from Banks Peninsula, as they headed eastwards towards dissolution and oblivion somewhere off Kaikoura.

❄ ❄ ❄

Wave scour. A dissolving iceberg.

Will ye no come back again?

Most icebergs that drift by on the Antarctic Circumpolar Current head up 'Iceberg Alley' to the east of the Campbell Plateau. But a few, and our recent visitors were among them, are pulled closer to land by local winds and currents.

Will we see their likes here again? Quite possibly, but it's been 70 years since the last icebergs were visible from mainland New Zealand, so it may be as long before the next one. However just because icebergs don't often drift into terrestrial view, doesn't mean they are not out there – over the horizon. In fact records of historical sightings by seafarers to the east of the South Island testify to that. And pre-historic records, by way of massive gouges on the sea floor of the Chatham Rise, show bergs passed by during the last ice age about 20,000 years ago.

We will remember our Antarctic visitors, in all their variety, with affection and awe. The stately tabular bergs sweeping by like giant aircraft carriers. The towering icy swans with their ghostly teal-blue keels beneath the waves. We marvelled at the aqua lakes and glistening cascades, the ice-boulder moonscapes, and the flock of floes bobbing by with them. It was a privilege to get acquainted with pilgrims of such ancient pedigree from such a far place and time. Do come by again. ❋

Shrek and his fleece on the Wools of New Zealand rug, wearing his aptly named Icebreaker coat.
Who else, but Southern Kiwis would pull such a stunt?

Glossary

calving – birth of an iceberg. When a chunk of ice breaks off an ice shelf or glacier, and floats free in the sea as an iceberg.

cetacean – an order of mammals including whales, porpoises and dolphins.

crampons – a spiky, metal plate fitted under footwear to provide grip on ice.

eddies – a circular or contrary motion of water at the side of the main current.

firn – a denser form of névé.

flotilla/armada – fleet.

flotsam – wreckage of a ship or cargo found floating on the surface of the water.

gyres – a circular movement, revolution, spiral or vortex.

isotope analysis – studying atomic neutrons in different samples of the same chemical to identify origin or provenance.

krill – a small shrimp-like crustacean.

merino – a breed of sheep prized for its fine wool.

millennium – a thousand years (plural 'millennia').

moraine – an area or bank of debris that a glacier or ice sheet has carried down and deposited.

nautical mile – 1852 metres.

névé – crystalline or granular snow on the upper part of a glacier.

shoal – an area of shallow water or submerged sandbank.

tsunami – tidal wave caused by an earthquake.

waratah – a metal fencing standard.

Dave Cull has lived in Dunedin for many years. He's a well-known television presenter and has fronted lifestyle and home improvement programmes since the 80s. He writes for several magazines and has published several lifestyle books, including *Vineyards on the Edge*, *The Great New Zealand Kitchen Book* and *Garden Landscaping*. His interests include fishing, gardening, wine, and developing a small horticultural block in Central Otago.

Stephen Jaquiery has worked as a newspaper photographer for over 27 years. He works as the Illustrations Editor at the *Otago Daily Times*. Stephen has won several awards for his work including the 2005 Qantas Newspaper Photographer of the Year Award. His photographs are widely published: his most recent book *City Birds* complemented an exhibition at the Otago Museum where a record 80,000 visitors flocked to view his stunning photographs.